SAD-VĀṆĪ-GĪTIKĀ

Philosophical essence of SAD-VĀṆĪ
through realization of
Swami Omkarananda Giri

SWA

SWA

The book is conceived, designed and edited by
Haimanti Bhattacharyya, founder of SWA
70, 3066 Eglinton Avenune West
Mississauga, Ontario, Canada
L5M 8E4

swa.theory@gmail.com

Published on: 17th Sep 2020
125th Birth Centenary of Ma Anandamayi

Author: Swami Omkarananda Giri
Translator: Haimanti Bhattacharyya
Publisher: Haimanti Bhattacharyya
Illustrator: Anirban Kanjilal
Acknowledgement: Dr. Manabendu Sarkar, Mr. Haran Naskar, Debashis Mukhopadhyay, Kalyan Moitra,

।।मातृ-अर्घ्य ।।

आनन्दमयि मातस्त्वं ब्रह्माणी वैष्णवी शिवा।
ऋक्-यजुः-साम-गायत्री त्वं हि वेदप्रकाशिका।
शिवशक्तिर्महामाया जगदम्बा त्रितापहा।
निमर्लोमा भवानी त्वं मातरर्घ्यं ग्रहाण मे।

- **स्वामी ओंकारानन्द गिरि**

mātṛ-arghya

ānandamayi mātastvaṁ brahmāṇī vaiṣṇavī śivā.
ṛk-yajuḥ-sāma-gāyatrī tvaṁ hi vedaprakāśikā.
śivaśaktirmahāmāyā jagadambā tritāpahā.
nimarlomā bhavānī tvaṁ mātararghyaṁ gṛhāṇa me.

- **Swami Omkarananda Giri**

BHAIJI WITH MA ANANDAMAYI

SAD-VĀṆĪ IS MA'S DIVINE TEACHING AS RECORDED BY BHAIJI

Foreword

Achievement of summum bonum is realized in yañja. On yajña Vedi 'Yāgñik' draws a triangle joining three points, which is called Yantra.

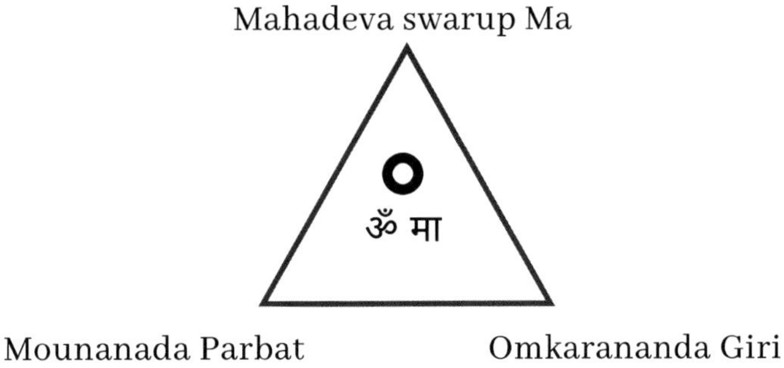

These shapes are psychological symbols corresponding to human consciousness. Here the composition of Sad-Vāṇī-Gītikā also may represent yajña. During the yajña, the central point of traditional yantras have a bindu or point, which represents the main deity, here (Aum)Pranava rupini Ma Anandamayi. The triangle pointing upwards is symbolic of the male principle (Purusha), here Mahadeva swarup Ma, portraying Ma Anandamayi's own expression of herself as "Purna brahma Narayan-Narayani, Mahadev-Mahadevi". On the base of the Yantra (Triangle), in the footsteps of Ma, two points are defining 'Sadhana' (spiritual practice). Those points represent Mounanada Parbat (Bhaiji) and Omkarananda Giri. One composed Ma's words as Sad-Vāṇī and the other expressed that vāṇīs in Sanskrit shlokas as Sad-Vāṇī-Gītikā. Sad-Vāṇī is The bridge to connect devotees with their inner soul, while Sad-Vāṇī-Gītikā is the gateway of the ultimate knowledge. Sad-Vāṇī-Gitīkā is not yet published. In order to make these Sanskrit shlokas accessible to the English knowing people, the book is getting published with English translation. Translator Haimanti is blessed with Vedantic sanyasi Omkarananda Giri's blessings and acquainted with the environment of Ma Anandamyi's direct followers from her childhood. She has studied Sanskrit and Vedas from Jadavpur University and presently she is an independent researcher on Indian Philosophy and Advaita Vedanta. I appreciate the effort from Haimanti, who translated Sad-Vāṇī-Gītikā for all readers. I offer the outcome of this effort to Ma's lotus feet. May the blessings remain with the effort of an ardent devotee of Ma Anandamayi.

Swami Mahananda Giri
15/09/2020

(Swami Mahananda Giri)

भूमिका

मातृचरणाश्रितः परमभक्तः आनन्दमयी इति आश्रमे भाइजी इति नाम्ना ख्यातः श्री ज्योतिषचन्द्रमहोदयः। तेन भक्तानां नित्यम् अनुध्येयं मातृकथामृतम् सद्-वाणी इति ग्रन्थे लिपिवद्धं कृतम्। इदं ग्रन्थम् एकाग्रचेतसा अनुध्यायन् ओंकारानन्दगिरिमहाराजोऽभिभूतः सञ्जातः। वाङमयी मा वेदस्वरूपा। तेन चिन्तितम् 'मातृकथा देवगिरा' एव लिखितव्या। 'आवृत्तिः सर्वशास्त्रानां वोधादपि गरीयसी' इत्युक्तम्। श्लोकेनैव भक्तजनानाम् आवृत्तिः सुकरा भवेत् इति विचिन्त्य तेन अनुष्टुभ्-छन्दसा श्लोकान् विरच्य सद्-वाणीनां मर्मकथाः अतिसंक्षेपेन ग्रथिताः। सद्-वाणीग्रन्थस्य प्रथमावाणी प्राणहीनं कर्म सर्वत्र पङ्गुताम् आनयति। सर्वकर्मनि प्राणसंयोगः एव मानवं लक्षे नयति। परिशेषे उक्तम्- प्राणपरिचयः सर्वेषां प्रत्यक्षगोचरः। तैत्तेरीयोपनिषदि उक्तम् 'नमस्ते वायो, त्वमेव प्रत्यक्षं व्रह्मासि'। प्राणावलम्बनमेव वुद्धेरपि अगोचरस्य सच्चिदानन्द- स्वरुपस्य उपलव्धेः सेतुस्वरूपम्। "sabsamay kheyal rakhate hobe pranbayu jemon amader byapokbhabete ek abicchinna royechhe-ini ke? ini amader sei satya chaitanyer ek rup, ei rupete prakash." (Bangmayi Ma, no-433)

सद्-वाणी ग्रन्थस्य मर्मकथा एकेनैव श्लोकेन महाराजेन ओंकारानन्देन लिखितम् –

"सद्-वाणी शतसंख्यया एकोत्तरेण केवलम्।
एकवाक्यं महावाक्यं प्राणप्रज्ञाविधायकम्।"

अस्मिन् प्रसङ्गे ओंकारानन्दगिरिमहाराजस्य जीवनादर्शः अस्माभिरनुध्येयः। पूर्वाश्रमे अवनीशङ्कर इति नाम्ना परिचित आत्ममर्यादा सपन्नो निष्ठावान् निरलसकर्मी स्वाधीनतासंग्रामी। तस्य सर्वम् आत्मवशं सुखम् इति आदर्श आसीत्।

“असक्तो ह्यचरन् कर्म परमाप्नोति पुरुषः” इति श्रीमद्भगवद्गीताया भगवतः उपदेशस्य स मूर्तप्रतीकः। संसारे सर्वकर्माणि अतिनिष्टया कुर्व्वन्नपि निर्लिप्तो निरासक्त आसीत्। वैदान्तशास्त्रे अधिकारिलक्षने उक्तम् ‘साधनचतुष्टयसम्पन्नः प्रमाता’। विवेकवैराग्यवान् स यथार्थ एव वेदान्तज्ञानस्य अधिकारी आसीत्। अगाधम् आसीत् तस्य पाण्डित्यम्। परन्तु सहजात वैराग्येन तेन मन्यते उपाधिर्व्यधिरेव। अतः नाम्ना सह तस्य पाण्डित्यपरिचायका उपाधयः कदापि न व्यवहृताः। शात्रानुशासनस्य व्यवहारिकप्रयोगे तस्य मननम् अनन्यसाधारणम् इति वहुजनैः उपलव्धम्। संग्राममयं जीवनम्। अविचलसत्यनिष्ठया अदम्यप्राणशक्त्या च स सर्वत्र जयी अभवत्। जीवनस्य वास्तवतया सह अध्यात्ममननस्य अपूर्वसंयोगः तस्य जीवनं महिममण्डितं कृतम्। स श्री श्री आनन्दमयीं मातरम् स्वीयगर्भधारिनीरूपेण संपश्य अभिभूतः सञ्जातः। मातुः समीपे तस्य आकुला प्रार्थना ‘Ma amake bhaijir gati dao’ जीवनसायाह्ने श्री श्री आनन्दमयी इति आश्रमस्य सन्यासी श्रीमच्चिन्मयानन्दगिरीमहाराजः sannyas to dirghadin-i hoye ache, vahirer aborantuku sudhu diye di’ – इत्युक्त्वा तं सन्न्यासमन्त्रेण दीक्षितवान्। जराशोकसन्तप्तजीवनेऽपि मातृकृपामग्नेन तेन उक्तम्ध न्योऽहं कृतकृत्योऽहं सफलं मम जीवनम्। तस्य अनुभूतिः – “Ma Bhagaban, Guru Bhagaban... Pai jeno antime taba pade sthan.”

- अपर्णा भट्टाचार्य
भूतपूर्व अध्यापिका

Introduction

'Sad-Vāṇī-Gītikā' is the fruit of meditation of Swami Omkarananda Giri. He intensely studied 'Sad-Vāṇī', a book written by Jyotis Chandra Roy, who is known as Bhaiji among Ma Anandamayi's followers. Bhaiji was one of the observants of Sri Sri Ma Anandamayi. He deeply contemplated Ma's every divine word within him and penned it as 'Sad-Vāṇī'. Swami Omkarananda Giri was amazed by reading this book. He realized that Ma's words are absolute knowledge and speech is divine teaching, so it needs to be expressed in Deva-bhasa (Sanskrit).

It says that 'even before understanding, recitation of knowledge is necessary'. Realizing that, Swami Omkarananda illustrated the summary of each vāṇī into shlokas by classical prosody "Anuṣtup". So that devotees could recite Ma's Sad-Vāṇī as daily prayer in the form of 'Sad-Vāṇī-Gītikā'.

The first vāṇī from Sad-Vāṇī is "In the field of action, people's minds become crippled... When the goal is ever before one as a living reality (Pranamay), all that is needful will come of its own accord". And at the end of Sad-Vāṇī, it says "one will come to realize that the individual is part of the One great life force..." Taittirīya Upaniṣad states that "namaste vāyo", "tvameva pratyakṣam brahmāsi" (bow to Thee, O Vayu! Thou indeed are the Perceptible Brahman).

'Tādātmya Bhāba' (relation of non-difference) which is beyond intellect, is like a bridge. Through the life force that relation reveals to sadhak and the relation between ultimate and jiva establishes. One hundred and one vāṇīs are composed in 'Sad-Vāṇī', which is being synopsized through shlokas as Sad-Vāṇī-Gītikā by Swami Omkarananda. Because the ultimate sentence (Mahāvākya) is always a single sentence to define consciousness. In this context, we should explore the philosophy of Swami Omkarananda's life. He was known by the name Abani Shankar before his spiritual renunciation. He was with tremendous self-esteem, dedicated to his work, truthful, and freedom fighter. He believed self-dependence is happiness. Gītā, says 'asakto hyacharankarma paramāpnoti'. He was the embodied impression of this śloka from Gītā.

In regular life. He did all his work sincerely being detached from worldly thoughts. As Vedanta's teaching, the seeker should be with four practices to pursue four stages (sādhanachatuṣtay). He was a conscientious monk and was perfectly competent in Vedantic knowledge. He believed degrees bring ego, despite having profound knowledge in Sanskrit and Indian philosophy and multiple academic degrees, because of his spontaneous abstinence he refrained from using any of his titles in the signature. Everybody observed his sincere performance of daily rites and disciplined lifestyle in every step. Though his life was full of struggle, he was always filled with the force of life, and being righteous he crossed all the hurdles in life.

Being a perfect follower of the Vedic 'four stages of life' ('Chaturāśrama'), his living was a beautiful combination of spirituality and practicality. After taking retirement from his teaching Life, when he came in association with Ma Anadamayi, he visualized "Ma" as his biological mother at first sight. His instance prayer before 'Ma' was "Ma amake Vaijir gati dao" (show me the same path as bhaiji). In the dusk of his life, he officially received renunciation from Swami Chinmoyananda Maharaj of Sri Sri Anandamayi ashram. Before renunciation, Chinmayanand Ji mentioned to him that, 'you are already in the mental state of renounce, throughout your life. Let me offer you the saffron'. Going through the physical pain and suffering of old age, he was in absolute bliss. He expressed his feelings through his song - 'Ma Bhagaban, Guru Bhagaban... Pai jeno antime taba pade sthan.' ('Ma you are the ultimate God, you are the ultimate Guru, wishing your Lotus feet at the end.')

- Aparna Bhattacharya
Former Professor

Preface

'There are many books on life and teachings of Sri Ma Anandamayi, 'Sad-Vāṇī' is one of them. 'Sad-Vāṇī-Gītikā' is the only philosophical research work done by swamiji on 'Sad-Vāṇī'. In my belief Ma is the ultimate God, and Ma's 'Sad-Vāṇī' is perfect spiritual teaching for our daily life. In last few months, as I started working on translating the manuscript of Swami Omkarananda Giri's Sad-Vāṇī-Gītikā', I realized how Swamiji contemplated Ma's teachings as ultimate with his deep philosophical realization and reflected those through shlokas. I was vastly enlightened by his enormous knowledge on Sanskrit language and Indian philosophy along with grammar, classical prosody. Swamiji's selection of words in each shloka established itself as 'Śabdabrahman'. Through 'Sad-Vāṇī-Gītikā', once again I realized how profound each word in Sanskrit is and why this language is called Devā-Bhasā. During this work, as I went through many queries, it cleared my thoughts and learning, and this work is one of the best life teachings for me.

Acknowledgments

Many well-wishers have guided and assisted me throughout this work, and I want to express my gratitude to them all, without their help the work might not have been possible. First I bow down to 'Pūrṇa-Brahman-swarūpiṇī' Ma, and to both Bhaiji and Swami Omkarananda Ji. My sincere bow to Swami Nirvanananda Ji for accepting this work through his sight. I bow to my guide and philosopher 'Swami Mahananda Giri and to My teacher prof. Aparna Bhattacharya for solving all my grammatical and philosophical queries. I am extremely missing the physical presence of Late Sanat Kumar Bandyopadhyay (author of Gītā-Śatakam and Śrīmad-Bhāgavatam in Bengali), who was very intimate to swami Omkarananda Giri and one of the prime teachers & guide during my academic career in Sanskrit.

My sincere bow to all senior Swamijis in Sri Sri Ma's order. I am blessed to have my mother's support, also it is Ma's grace to get my father alongside me throughout the journey and guiding me in the perfect way. Thankful to Udita Bhattacharyya for her support. This work would not have been possible without their presence and blessings. My heartfelt gratitude to Mr. Kalyan Moitra for his initial effort and to Mr. Debashis Mukhopadhyay for his guidance.

I acknowledge Dr. Manabendu Sarkar (Assistant Professor, Department of Sanskrit, Vivekananda College, Thakurpukur, Kolkata) and Mr. Haran Naskar (Project Assistant, Department of Sanskrit, Jadavpur University) for their sincere effort on the complete work of Devanagari scripting and Transliteration of shlokas. We put our best effort to publish Sad-Vāṇī-Gītikā', a deep meditating work of Swami Omkarananda Giri.

"I take refuge in the Self, the Indivisible, the Existence-Consciousness-Bliss Absolute, beyond the reach of words and thought, and the Substratum of all, for the attainment of my cherished desire."

- *Vedāntasāra.*

- Haimanti Bhattacharyya

(Publisher and Translator)

सद्-वाणी शतसंख्याया एकोत्तरेण केवलम्।
एकवाक्यं महावाक्यं प्राणप्रज्ञा विधायकम्।।

SAD-VĀṆĪ-GĪTIKĀ

स्वाधीन-गति-हीनानाम्,
पङ्गुत्वं साध्य-साधनम्।
प्राणमय-प्रयासेन
लक्ष्यं स्वयम् इवागतम्।।१।।

svādhīna-gati-hīnānām,
paṅgutvaṁ sādhya-sādhanam.
prāṇamaya-prayāsena
lakṣyaṁ svayam ivāgatam.

The seeker's ability to seek a target, gets crippled due to absence of free force of will. By devoted endeavor, the target (almighty) appears itself. (1)

आकृष्टा-कर्षक-द्वैतम्
तादात्म्य-भाव-मण्डितम्।
निर्मलंयावद् आकृष्टं,
आकर्षणं भवेद् ध्रुवम्।।२।।

ākṛṣṭā-karṣaka-dvaitam
tādātmya-bhāva-maṇḍitam.
nirmalaṁyāvad ākṛṣṭaṁ,
ākarṣaṇaṁ bhaved dhruvam.

Both attracted and attractor are connected with 'tādātmya-bhāba' (relation of non-difference) in state of trance. When attracted is pure, then attraction is obvious. (2)

ससीमा-सीमयोर्ज्ञानम्।
अनेकम् एककान्वितम्।
एकस्यैव च वाहुल्यम्
तत्परिणतम् एककम्।।३।।

sasīmā-sīmayorjñānam.
anekam ekakānvitam.
ekasyaiva ca vāhulyam
tatpariṇatam ekakam.

The knowledge of finite and infinite is unified within one. One diverges in many and many conclude to one. (3)

एकतो दशम स्थानम्
साध्य-सोपान-संख्यकम्।
आरुढो दशमं स्थानम्
आनयेत् साध्य-सिद्धताम्।।४।।

ekato daśama sthānam
sādhya-sopāna-saṁkhyakam.
āruḍho daśamaṁ sthānam
ānayet sādhya-siddhatām.

There are ten sequential stages to reach the ascetic's target (self-realization). By reaching the tenth stage, the seeker attains his fruition. (4)

परमानन्द-लाभाय
भगवत्-शरणागतम्।
लब्धञ्चहि तद् आनन्दं
दुःखैर्यावत् विशीर्णकम्।।५।।

paramānanda-lābhāya
bhagavat-śaraṇāgatam.
labdhañcahi tad ānandaṁ
duḥkhairyābat viśīrṇakam.

To realize blissfulness, have recourse to almighty. By obtaining that happiness all sufferings diminish. (5)

याच्ञा हि दर्शनं यस्मै
प्राप्तव्यं तस्य दर्शनम्।
एकान्त प्रार्थनायां स
वर्त्तते ते समीपकम्।।६।।

yāñcā hi darśanaṁ yasmai
prāptavyaṁ tasya darśanam.
ekānta prārthanāyāṁ sa
varttate te samīpakam.

Seek His holy appearance, and you will obtain that. Through intense prayer, He remains near to the seeker. (6)

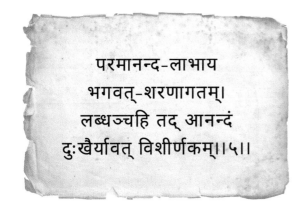

स्रष्टुः सृष्टम् इदम् विश्वम्
किञ्चिदपि न दूषितम्।
सर्वं तावत् श्रियायुक्तं
हृदयं चेत् श्रियान्वितम्।।७।।

sraṣṭuḥ sṛṣṭam idam viśvam
kiṇcidapi na dūṣitam.
sarvaṁ tāvat śriyāyuktaṁ
hṛdayaṁ cet śriyānvitam.

There is nothing impure in this universe, created by the creator.If your heart is full of grace, then everything appears graceful. 7

प्राण प्रियं यदा सर्वम्
महोत्सव निकेतनम्।
आनन्दस्य प्रभावेन
सर्वानन्दं हि मामकम्।।८।।

prāṇa priyaṁ yadā sarvam
mahotsava niketanam.
ānandasya prabhāvena
sarvānandaṁ hi māmakam.

When all is your beloved, it becomes a manifestation of supreme joy. Through the effect of that happiness, everyone's joy turns into self-happiness. 8

एकतो जायते सर्वम्
वहुधा च प्रतिष्ठितम्।
पृथक् पृथक् स्थितिस्थानं
गन्तव्यं तु तद् एककम्।।९।।

ekato jāyate sarvam
vahudhā ca pratiṣṭhitam.
pṛthak pṛthak sthitisthānaṁ
gantavyaṁ tu tad ekakam

All emerge from one and establish in many. Their state of life is different but the destination is that one. (9)

सेवाभावो प्रभौ दासे
सेवा तावन्नहि द्वयम्।
सेवा धर्मो हि दासस्य
सेव्यता च प्रभुत्वके।।१०।।

sevābhāvo prabhau dāse
sevā tāvannahi dvayam.
sevā dharmo hi dāsasya
sevyatā ca prabhutvake.

The act of service between divine and devotee is not dual. The duty of a devotee is service and through his spirit of service, he integrates into divinity. (10)

आनन्द-लेशमात्रेण
जनानां तद्दिनं गतम्।
मूलं जिङ्गासुभि स्तस्मै
कृत्यं तत् साध्य-साधनम्।।११।।

ānanda-leśamātreṇa
janānāṁ taddinaṁ gatam.
mūlaṁ jiṅgāsubhi stasmai
kṛtyaṁ tat sādhya-sādhanam.

Common people are living their days only with least happiness. By actively seeking the ultimate knowledge, they obtain the goal. (11)

सुखे दुःखे सदामग्नं
संसारिणाञ्च मानसम्।
पवित्र-मनसा प्राप्यं
योगिनामपि दुर्लभम्।।१२।।

sukhe duḥkhe sadāmagnaṁ
saṁsāriṇāñca mānasam.
pavitra-manasā prāpyaṁ
yogināmapi durlabham.

The mind of ordinary men is always engrossed in weal and woe. Which is even rare to yogis, people can attain that through pure mind. (12)

अलस-मनसः कार्यं
कुत्रापि न च तत्परम्।
भवेत्प्राणप्रियं कृत्यम्
तावत् कार्य्यं सुसाधनम्।।१३।।

alasa-manasaḥ kāryaṁ
kutrāpi na ca tatparam.
bhavetprāṇapriyaṁ kṛtyam
tāvat kāryyaṁ susādhanam.

Work performed with a slothful mind never expedites. When work is performed with passion, the action is accomplished perfectly. (13)

आनन्दजमनस्तावत्
शत्रुमित्रादि कारणम्।
त्यज शत्रुभावं सर्वम्
परिष्फोटय मित्रताम्।।१४।।

ānandajamanastāvat
śatrumitrādi kāraṇam.
tyaja śatrubhāvaṁ sarvam
pariṣphotaya mitratām.

Where the mind emerged from perfect happiness then why there is an enemy or friend? By abandoning the animus, always friendliness unfolds. (14)

अन्तर्वहिः समीकृत्य
धर्म-कर्म-समाचरण्।
शुभोदये च तद् दृष्टम्
उभयोः समरूपकम्।।१५।।

antarvahiḥ samīkṛtya
dharma-karma-samācaraṇ.
śubhodaye ca tad driṣṭam
ubhayoḥ samarūpakam.

Conduct both spiritual and worldly acts by unifying your inward and outward world. Equality appears when goodness arises through that vision. 15

सत्ये प्रतिष्ठितस्यैव
सात्त्विकत्वं समागतम्।
आहारे सात्त्विकत्वञ्च
सत्येनैव प्रतिष्ठितम्।।१६।।

satye pratiṣṭhitasyaiva
sāttvikatvaṁ samāgatam.
āhāre sāttvikatvañca
satyenaiva pratiṣṭhitam.

Purity (sāttvicatā) appears to him, who is manifested in the truth. When one's life is established on truth, even purity (sāttvictā) of food is manifested within that truth. 16

साधक-जीवनं पूर्णम्
महताह्वानम् आगतम्।
सर्वैः प्राप्यं तद् आह्वानम्
जीव-शिव-कथामृतम्।।१७।।

sādhaka-jīvanaṁ pūrṇam
mahatāhvānam āgatam.
sarvaiḥ prāpyaṁ tad āhvānam
jīva-śiva-kathāmṛtam.

The life of a seeker is complete when the ultimate invocation appears. By receiving that invocation, the gospel of creature and almighty establishes. (17)

स्व-सम्मान प्रतीक्षायै
कटाक्षं तव नोचितम्।
सश्रद्धं प्रेम जानीहि
भगवान् प्राप्यते ध्रुवम्।।१८।।

sva-sammāna pratīkṣāyai
kaṭākṣaṁ tava nocitam.
saśraddhaṁ prema jānīhi
bhagavān prāpyate dhruvam.

For exposing self-honor, one should not sneer. If there is love and gratitude, attainment of God is certain. (18)

एकतो जायते विश्वम्
एकेनैव प्रतिष्ठितम्।
एकस्मिन्नेव संलीनम्
एकमेवाद्वितीयकम्।।१९।।

ekato jāyate viśvam
ekenaiva pratiṣṭhitam.
ekasminneva saṁlīnam
ekamevādvitīyakam.

Cosmos originated from one. Established into oneness and immersed in the same. Only one is there, not two. (19)

तर्कातीतं भवेद् वाक्यम्
स्वल्पं तथाच वक्तव्यम्।
शक्तौ वृद्धिं गतायां हि
तर्कंभवेद् विशीर्णकम्।।२०।।

tarkātītaṁ bhaved vākyam
svalpaṁ tathāca vaktavyam.
śaktau vṛddhiṁ gatāyāṁ hi
tarkaṁbhaved viśīrṇakam.

The articulation should be concise, and the speech undebatable. Through increased competency, chatter will be reduced. (20)

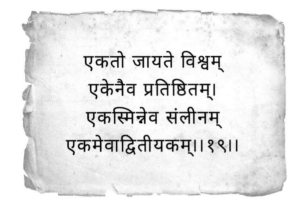

साहसोत्साह-शक्तीनां
कर्मिणाञ्च त्रयान्वितम्।
साफल्यम् अन्यथा तेषां
पतनम् अनिवार्य्यकम्।।२१।।

sāhasotsāha-śaktīnāṁ
karmiṇāñca trayānvitam.
sāphalyam anyathā teṣāṁ
patanam anivāryyakam

The pursuers can succeed if they have the combination of the trio- courage, enthusiasm, and power. Otherwise, their fall is certain. (21)

अनित्य-देह-वद्धा चित्
प्राप्नोति क्रमपङ्गुताम्।
मुक्ताञ्चलं चिदाकाशं
आत्मनः स्वनिकेतनम्।।२२।।

anitya-deha-vaddhā chit
prāpnoti kramapaṅgutām.
muktāñcalaṁ cidākāśaṁ
ātmanaḥ svaniketanam.

Confined Consciousness in the mortal body slowly becomes disable. Free 'cosmic space of consciousness' is the real space of self. (22)

विद्यमाने ममत्वे हि
न लभ्यं स्वात्म-चिन्तनम्।
तदाकृष्टस्य तस्यैव
सम्भवेत् स्वात्मदर्शनम्।।२३।।

vidyamāne mamatve hi
na labhyaṁ svātma-cintanam.
tadākṛṣṭasya tasyaiva
sambhavet svātmadarśanam.

In the presence of ‘affection to I’, self-thinking is not attainble. With the attraction of His grace, self-observation can be realized. (23)

विषयासक्तमात्रेण
न भवेत् स्वात्मचिन्तनम्।
आचित्तशुद्धि नेतव्यं
सत्सङ्गाद् आत्मचिन्तनम्।।२४।।

viṣayāsaktamātreṇa
na bhavet svātmacintanam.
ācittaśuddhi netavyaṁ
satsaṅgād ātmacintanam.

A materialistic personality can not perform self-thinking. To obtain self-realization, acquire mind purification from the holy association. (24)

विवेकिनां सदासत्यं
पूर्णं करोति जीवनम्।
लब्धवान् हि गुणग्राही
पतनं दोषदर्शिनाम्।।२५।।

vivekināṁ sadāsatyaṁ
pūrṇaṁ karoti jīvanam.
labdhavān hi guṇagrāhī
patanaṁ doṣadarśinām.

A conscientious person's life fulfills through everlasting honesty. One is benefited by being an appreciator, while critics deteriorate. (25)

सत् चिन्तने मनुष्यत्वम्
सत् स्वरूपं प्रकाशितम्।
सत्यं सज्जीवनं पूर्णं
मानवत्वञ्च सार्थकम्।।२६।।

sat cintane manuṣyatvam
sat svarūpaṁ prakāśitam.
satyaṁ sajjīvanaṁ pūrṇaṁ
mānavatvañca sārthakam.

True nature of humanity reveals through pure thought. The completeness of human life appears through truthful noble living. (26)

आनन्दाज्जायते विश्वम्
आनन्दमयतामिदम्।
प्राप्तं तद् आनन्दं सत्यम्
वाङ्-मनसोरगोचरम्।।२७।।

ānandājjāyate viŚvam
ānandamayatāmidam.
prāptaṁ tad ānandaṁ satyaṁ
bāṅ-manasoragocaram.

The universe is evolved from eternal joy and it's filled with the same happiness. By obtaining that true bliss, the soul reaches, beyond the speech and mind. 27

अप्रत्यक्षं स्वनेत्रेन
स्वकीय-मूर्त्ति-दर्शनम्।
निन्दा-स्तुति-द्वयोरूर्द्धं
स्थातव्यम् एक लक्ष्यकम्।।२८।।

apratyakṣaṁ svanetrena
svakīya-mūrtti-darŚanam.
nindā-stuti-dvayorūrddhaṁ
sthātavyam eka lakṣyakam.

Self-visualization is possible through the inner eye. Beyond both praise and criticism, one settles himself to the goal. 28

तत् चिन्तामणिम् आदाय
तन्मय भाव-भावनम्।
चिन्तामुक्तं करोति सः
तस्यैव शरणागतम्।।२९।।

tat cintāmaṇim ādāya
tanmaya bhāva-bhāvanam.
cintāmuktaṁ karoti saḥ
tasaiyava śaraṇāgatam.

Contemplate being quiet in thoughts of Chintāmani(full filler of desires or God). He sets free all worries if one can devote all thoughts to Him. (29)

भवेत् प्राणमयं हास्यं
अन्तर्वहिः समीकृतम्।
जगज्जयि भवेद् हास्यं
तच्चरणे विलग्नकम्।।३०।।

bhavet prāṇamayaṁ hāsyaṁ
antarvahiḥ samīkṛtam.
jagajjayi bhaved hāsyaṁ
taccaraṇe vilagnakam.

When your inside and out unites to spontaneous laughter, then the Laughter will conquer the whole world. Keep yourself surrendering to His lotus feet. (30)

सहमानः स्वपीडाञ्च
सेवमानः स्वदेहकम्।
प्रतिवेशी तथा सेव्यः
भवेद् एकात्म-साधनम्।।३१।।

sahamānaḥ svapīḍāñca
sevamānaḥ svadehakam.
prativeśī tathā sevyaḥ
bhaved ekātma-sādhanam.

The way you accept your physical pain and take care of it. Similarly serving others with the feeling of oneness leads to unification. (31)

मनस उपासना मात्रं
प्राणमयं हि भावनम्
मनःस्थिरं भवेत् सत्यम्,
तत् कृपावारि लब्धकम्।।३२।।

manasa upāsanā mātraṁ
prāṇamayaṁ hi bhāvanam.
manaḥsthīraṁ bhavet satyam
tat kṛpāvāri labdhakam.

Thought becomes vibrant through mental worship. The shower of grace is attained only when the mind is still. (32)

स्रष्टुः सृष्टं नृरूपत्वं
नरत्वम् ईश रूपकम्।
मनोरत्नाकरे रत्नं
साधनेन तदात्मकम्।।३३।।

sraṣṭuḥ sṛṣṭaṁ nṛrūpatvaṁ
naratvam īśa rūpakam.
manoratnākare ratnaṁ
sādhanena tadātmakam.

Man is the creation of the creator, also that man is the image of the creator. Through spiritual practice in deep down the mind, the ultimate jewel is obtained. (33)

भाषया प्रकाश्यं सर्वम्
मनोगतञ्च भावनम्।
उपलब्धं तद् आनन्दं
वाङ्-मनसोरगोचरम्।।३४।।

bhāṣayā prakāśyaṁ sarvam
manogatañca bhāvanam.
upalabdhaṁ tad ānandaṁ
bāṅ-manasoragocaram.

Psychic feelings are always revealed by language. 'That' true happiness, which is realized, is beyond thoughts and words. (34)

अस्ति नास्ति च तत्सत्यम्
सर्वव्यापि न दर्शनम्।
सर्वत्र तद् अवस्थानम्
योगदृष्ट्या तु केवलम्।।३५।।

asti nāsti ca tatsatyam
sarvavyāpi na darśanam.
sarvatra tad avasthānam
yogdṛṣṭyā tu kevalam.

Both the existence and non-existence are true, and though being omnipresent He doesn't always appear. Only through the yogic vision, His presence can be realized. (35)

शूण्यं शुभ्रं अरूपं वा
शूण्यं तत् सर्वरूपकम्।
आत्माभिमान-शूण्यंत्वं
सर्वरूप-समागमम्।।३६।।

śūṇyaṁ śubhraṁ arūpaṁ vā
śūṇyaṁ tat sarvarūpakam.
ātmābhimāna-śūnyatvaṁ
sarvarūpa-samāgamam.

Pure, transparent, and formless He pervades in the void. In the void of self-conceit, his all appearances assemble. (36)

स्रोतस्विनी-गति-स्तुल्यं
लक्ष्यञ्च दुर्णिवारितम्।
साधकस्य तथा लक्ष्यं
परमतत्त्व-साधनम्।।३७।।

srotasvinī-gati-stulyaṁ
lakṣyañca durṇivāritam.
sādhakasya tathā lakṣyaṁ
paramatattva-sādhanam.

The focus of a seeker to obtain the ultimate knowledge is comparable to an irresistible torrent towards its destination. 37

नमामि परमं हंसम्
येन तदात्म दर्शनम्।
आत्म-सम्वन्धतः सत्यम्
शिष्य आत्मज रूपकम्।।३८।।

namāmi paramaṁ haṁsam
yena tadātma darśanam.
ātma-samvandhataḥ satyam
śiṣya ātmaja rūpakam.

By taking a bow to the enlightened, perceive your true self within Him. The disciple is like his own child. The relation between souls is the only truth. 38

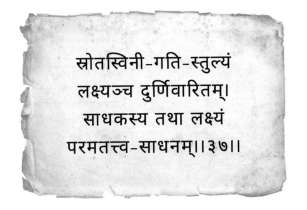

सुनीतौ धर्मराजत्वं
सत्यं तत्र प्रतिष्ठितम्।
शाधि च प्राक्मनोराज्यं
स्वाराज्यं स्वयम् आगतम्।।३९।।

sunītau dharmarājatvaṁ
satyaṁ tatra pratiṣṭhitam.
śādhi ca prākmanorājyaṁ
svārājyaṁ svayam āgatam.

Truth holds upon the religious domain. First, take control of your mind, His heavenly abode appears itself. 39

देह-यन्त्र-निरीक्षार्थं
आयुर्वेद-निरीक्षणम्।
अन्तर्यामि-निरीक्षायै
जगच्चित्रस्य दर्शनम्।।४०।।

deha-yantra-nirīkṣārthaṁ
āyurveda-nirīkṣaṇam.
antaryāmi-nirīkṣāyai
jagaccitrasya darśanam.

Ayurveda is practiced for inspection of the human body. Likewise through exploring the indweller, impression of the physical world can be sighted. 40

योग-ध्यान-समाधिभ्य:
संकीर्त्तणं सुसाधनम्।
यस्मैच नाम कीर्त्तनम्
तत्-स्मर्त्तव्यं हि केवलम्।।४१।।

yoga-dhyāna-samādhibhyaḥ
saṁkīrttaṇaṁ susādhanam.
yasmaica nāma kīrttanam
tat-smarttavyaṁ hi kevalam.

Yoga meditation or absorption is more austere than a musical congregation. Down the lane of this blissful music, the deity only pervades in the mind. (41)

अहं कर्त्तेति मूढत्वं,
भवेश्च द्वन्द्व-शूण्यता।
अहं कर्त्ता गुणाधीन:
यो न वेत्ति जगत्-पतिम्।।४२।।

ahaṁ kartteti mūḍhatvaṁ,
bhaveśca dvandva-śūṇyatā.
āhaṁ karttā guṇādhīnaḥ
yo na vetti jagat-patim.

He is ignorant who thinks himself the doer or master. Conflict of impermanence resolves through the knowledge that 'He is the only master', who is beyond all the qualities. 'I', the ignorant, is covered with the qualities. (42)

वलं देहि वृथा याच्ञा
त्वयि तत् विद्यते वलम्।
विश्वासेन प्रयासेन
वलं स्वयं प्रकाशितम्।।४३।।

valaṁ dehi bṛthā yāñcā
tvayi tat vidyate valam.
viśvāsena prayāsena
valaṁ svayaṁ prakāśitam.

Asking for power is only in vain. The power is within you. With the faith and strive, power reveals itself. (43)

श्रवने मनने ब्रह्म
सत्यमेकं समाहितं।
सर्वमिदं खलु ब्रह्म
सर्वेषामन्तरात्मकम्।।४४।।

śravane manane brahma
satyamekaṁ samāhitaṁ.
sarvamidaṁ khalu brahma
sarveṣāmantarātmakam.

Listening to spiritual teaching, and meditating upon Brahaman, reveals that the truth is embodied in one. All this is Brahman and so is everyone's inner soul. (44)

शान्ति स्थानं सुदुर्लभम्
विश्वमिदम् अपूर्णकम्।
शान्ति स्थानं तद् आनन्दम्
चिदाकाशे विराजितम्।।४५।।

śānti sthānaṁ sudurlabham
viśvamidam apūrṇakam.
śānti sthānaṁ tad ānandam
cidākāśe virājitam.

Serenity and peace are rare in this incomplete volatile world. Peace and pure happiness belongs to the sky of consciousness. (45)

स्मरेन् नित्मम् अनित्यत्वम्,
जातस्य मरणं ध्रुवम्।
विशुद्ध-चेतसा नित्यम्,
कुरु तद् आत्मदर्शनम्।।४६।।

smaren nityam anityatvam,
jātasya maraṇaṁ dhruvam.
biśuddha-cetasā nityam,
kuru tad ātmadarśanam.

Always keep it in remembrance of what is not permanent. Both birth and death are eternal truth. With a pure heart observe your true Self. (46)

सत् कर्मिणां सदिच्छायाम्
तद् वलं स्वयम् आगतम्।
पवित्र हृदये तेषां
कर्मिणाम् आत्मदर्शनम्।।४७।।

sat karmiṇāṁ sadicchāyām
tad valaṁ svayaṁ āgatam.
pavitra hṛdaye teṣāṁ
karmiṇām ātmadarśanam.

By the pure desire of a perfect seeker, the true power appears by itself. He also experiences the self with a transcendent heart. (47)

अखन्ड-खन्ड-रूपेण
महाकालस्य रूपकम्।
नित्यानित्यविवेकेन
एकं हि न द्वितीयकम्।।४८।।

akhanḍa-khanḍa-rūpeṇa
mahākālasya rūpakam.
nityānityavivekena
ekaṁ hi na dvitīyakam.

Both the 'manifested in many' and 'whole' are the appearances of 'Mahākāla'(the great God beyond time). It is only realized by the true knowledge of permanent and transient, that there is only one, not two. (48)

सेव्य-सेवक-सेवायाम्
कर्म-कर्त्तृ-क्रियाफलम्।
काय-मनो-वचस्त्रिभिः
सेवा चात्मसमर्पणम्।।४९।।

sevya-sevaka sevāyām
karma-karttṛ-kriyāphalam.
kāya-mano-bacāsthribhiḥ
sevā cātmasamarpaṇam.

The service itself, both who is giving and receiving the service, along with the good work, the doer, and the result, all are the same. It is the ultimate surrender when service is provided by the body, mind, and speech altogether. (49)

विगत संशयो यस्मात्
विश्वास इति लब्धकम्।
विश्वासो गुरुषु श्रद्धा
तस्यां सत्यं प्रकाशितम्।।५०।।

vigata saṁśayo yasmāt
viśvāsa iti labdhakam.
viśvāso guruṣu śraddhā
tasyāṁ satyaṁ prakāśitam.

Doubt goes away when faith is strong. When there is belief and faith in the teacher, then only the real truth reveals itself. (50)

सर्वदर्शिणि पूर्णत्वं
तत्पश्येद् जगदीश्वरम्।
सद्-वाणीनीयतांनित्यं
ध्यायन्नित्यं तन्नामकम्।।५१।।

sarvadarśiṇi pūrṇatvaṁ
tatpaśyed jagadīśavaram.
sad-vāṇīnīyatāṁnityaṁ
dhyāyannityaṁ tannāmakam.

He, the ultimate, is omniscient and he is God. Know him, meditate upon his name, and remember his spiritual speech in every moment of your life. (51)

कालक्षयि सुखं भूयः
भवेद् दुःखस्य कारणम्
मेघमुक्तं चिदाकाशम्
चिरशान्ति-निकेतनम्।।५२।।

kālakṣayi sukhaṁ bhūyaḥ
bhaved duḥkhasya kāraṇam.
meghamuktaṁ cidākāśam
ciraśānti-niketanam.

By the journey of time, the same happiness becomes the cause of suffering. Eternal peace resides within the clear sky of Consciousnes. (52)

गतिशीलं जगन् नित्यं
सुखं दुःखं क्रमागतम्।
शान्तिपूर्णं भवेन् नित्यं
मा-गुरु-चरणं ध्रुवम्।।५३।।

gatiśīlaṁ jagan nityaṁ
sukhaṁ duḥkhaṁ kramāgatam.
śāntipūrṇaṁ bhaven nityaṁ
mā-guru-caraṇaṁ dhruvam.

The world is moving forward with periodic joy and misery. Ultimate peace is attained when one takes shelter under Ma's lotus feet. (53)

आत्म समीक्षया नित्यं
आत्मानं कुरु संस्कृतम्।
कर्मणि शुद्ध भावेन
धर्म कर्म सुसाधनम्।।५४।।

ātma samīkṣayā nityaṁ
ātmānaṁ kuru saṁskṛtam.
karmaṇi śuddha bhāvena
dharma karma susādhanam.

Self-purification comes by continual self-analyzation. When your work is dedicated with a pure insight, your all religious activity will be perfectly complete. (54)

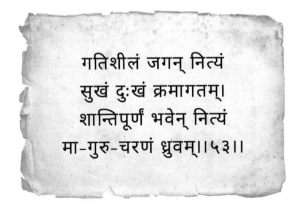

ब्रह्मान्ड कल्पो देहोऽयम्
नित्यानित्य-विमिश्रितम्।
आत्मरतिं विना देहे
सर्वं शून्यं निरीक्षितम्।।५५।।

brahmāṇḍa kalpo deho 'yam
nityānitya-vimiśritam.
ātmaratiṁ binā dehe
sarvaṁ śūnyaṁ nirīkṣitam.

The body can be imagined as the universe, where both are combination of permanent and transient things. Going beyond all the senses of the gross body and being absorbed within the self one could perceive the void. (55)

तद् ब्रह्म यच्च दुर्ज्ञेयं
विद्यया तच्च दुर्गमम्।
आनन्दस्य प्रतीकेन
तद् ध्यानेन सुगम्यताम्।।५६।।

tad brahma yacca durjñeyaṁ
vidyayā tacca durgamam.
ānandasya pratīkena
tad dhyānena sugamyatām.

The brahman is beyond the reach, even difficult to understand through knowledge. The brahman is the symbol of true happiness, and He reveals through the meditation on that particular joy. (56)

तज्ज्योतिर्भगवत्प्रेम
सतसङ्गात् गृहं नीयताम्।
गृहलक्ष्मीर्भवेज्ज्योतिः
ज्योतिर्मयं गृहंगृहम्।।
पूर्णमदः इदं पूर्णं
सुस्वागतं सनातनम्।।५७।।

tajjyotirbhagavatprema
satsaṅgāt gṛhaṁ nīyatām.
gṛhalakṣmīrbhavejjyotiḥ
jyotirmayaṁ gṛhaṁgṛham.
pūrṇamadaḥ idaṁ pūrṇaṁ
susvāgataṁ sanātanam.

His divine glow lightens those places where eternal love and ascetic companions are always in spiritual practice. These dwellings get illuminated by the lights of the goddess Laxmi. That completeness and this completeness welcomes the Sanātana. (57)

सर्वसंकल्प-मुक्तस्य
सर्वत्यागाच्च निश्चितम्।
शून्यस्थान-निवासाच्च
सन्न्यासिनं नता वयम्।।५८।।

sarvasaṁkalpa-muktasya
sarvatyāgācca niścitam.
śūnyasthāna-nivāsācca
sannyāsinaṁ natā bayam.

Who is free from all wishes, is certain to renounce all desires. He settles in the void and he is the true monk. (58)

समुद्र-पर्व्वतौ द्वैतम्
स्वात्म-चिन्तालय-द्वयम्।
भावलक्ष्यं तरङ्गत्वे
पर्वते नीरवत्वकम्।।५९।।

samudra-parvvatau dvaitam
svātma-cintālaya-dvayam.
bhāvalakṣyaṁ taraṅgatve
parvate nīravatvakam.

Seashore and mountain both are the perfect places for introspection. Emotions focus on the waves and the silence remains in the mountain. 59

अहंकार-विनाशकं
साधकं शरनागतम्।
मातृपदं नयेत् शीघ्रं
सद्-गुरुर्हि केवलम्।।६०।।

ahaṁkāra-vināśakaṁ
sādhakaṁ śaranāgatam.
mātṛpadaṁ nayet śīghraṁ
sad-gururhi kevalam.

Seeker (sādhaka) remains in total surrender by eliminating his ego. One obtains Ma's lotus feet, following a true spiritual teacher. 60

कर्म-भाव-द्वयोर्मध्ये
तावद् उत्सश्च भावनम्।
प्रेयः श्रेयो द्वयोः श्रेयः
अन्तीमे सुखकारणम्।।६१।।

karma-bhāva-dvayarmadhye
tāvad utsaśca bhāvanam.
preyaḥ śreyo dvayoḥ śreyaḥ
āntīme sukhakāraṇam.

The origin of both action and emotion is only the psychic world. Between pleasure (Preya) and perennial joy (Shreya), the last one is the ultimate cause of happiness. 61

प्रायशश्जरया वृद्धौ
संकुचितं मनोगतम्।
विश्वप्रेम्ना वलिष्टश्च
दर्शनीयः स केवलम्।।६२।।

prāyaśaśjarayā bṛddhau
saṁkucitaṁ manogatam.
biśvapremnā valiṣṭaśca
darśanīyaḥ sa kevalam.

The senescence of old age turns morale down, but an approach of universal love makes one debonair. 62

विरहे मिलनेच्छायां
तावत् सुखं समागतम्।
शरणागतमात्रेषु
नित्यानन्दं विराजितम्।।६३।।

virahe milanecchāyāṁ
tābat sukhaṁ samāgatam.
śaraṇāgatamātreṣu
nityānandaṁ birājitam.

The desire to reconcile in separation brings a shower of joy. True happiness is within the total surrender. (63)

इच्छया नेच्छया वापि
त्रिताप दग्धजीवनम्
गतं तावन्निरानन्दम्
तन्नामकीर्त्तनैर्ध्रुवम्।।६४।।

icchayā necchayā vāpi
tritāpa dagdhajīvanam.
gataṁ tavannirānandam
tannāmakīrttanairdhruvam.

Willingly or unwillingly, life is always in three forms of travails and suffering (tritāpa). All sorrows could go away by only reciting His supreme name. (64)

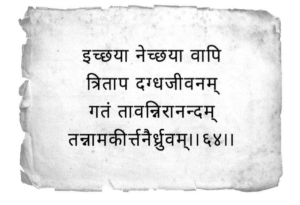

जगत्-व्यापि-कृपा तस्य
तत् कृपाहि केवलम्
शुद्ध-भाव-क्रिया-प्राप्तम्
तस्य प्रत्यक्ष दर्शनम्।।६५।।

jagat-vyāpi-kṛpā tasya
tat kṛpāhi kevalam.
śuddha-bhāva-kriyā-prāptam
tasya pratyakṣa darśanam.

His blessings are evermore dwelling over the world and His grace is the ultimate. He reflects himself through the work with a pure mind. 65

वृहत् पापं हि दौर्वल्यम्
शक्तिक्षयस्य कारणम्।
देह-मनः-सुसन्धाने
आत्म सन्धान साधनम्।।६६।।

vṛhat pāpaṁ hi daurvalyam
śaktikṣayasya kāraṇam.
deha-manaḥ-susandhāne
ātma sandhāna sādhanam.

Weakness is the most sin and it leads to deterioration of power. By taking care of body-mind, self-query arises. 66

अविरामं स्मरेन्नाम
तस्य नाम हि केवलम्।
श्वास-प्रश्वास युक्तेन
तन्नाम्ना सर्वसिद्धिदम्।।६७।।

avirāmaṁ smarennām
tasya nāma hi kevalam.
śvāsa-praśvāsa yuktena
tannāmnā sarvasiddhidam.

Continuously practice the supreme name, His name is the only truth. When the name unites with every bit of breath, complete attainment happens. (67)

उच्छवासे भावप्रकाशः
तच्च जपादि-साधनम्।
साध्य-साधक-सम्बन्धः
तद् भावनं हि केवलम्।।६८।।

ucchvāse bhāvaprakāśaḥ
tacca japādi-sādhanam.
sādhya-sādhaka-sambandhaḥ
tad bhāvanaṁ hi kevalam.

An ecstatic emotion, spiritual practice, and repetition of a mantra is a manifestation of devotional feeling. The relation between a devotee and his aim is only the cogitation of God. (68)

भोग-मोक्ष-द्वय-क्षेत्रम्
इच्छाशक्ते रहं कृतम्
अन्तर्यामि विचारेण
अहं नाम्ना विलुप्तकम्।।६९।।

bhoga-mokṣa-dvaya-kṣetram
īcchāśakte rahaṁ kṛtam.
antaryāmi vicāreṇa
āhaṁ nāmnā biluptakam.

For both pleasure and liberation will power appears as ego. Through the path of self-query, the "feeling of I' disappears. (69)

संसारे भोग सर्वस्वे
कोषागारस्य रिक्तताम्।
दृष्टाय मन्यते व्यर्थं
मानवानां हि जीवनम्।।७०।।

saṁsāre bhoga sarvasve
koṣāgārasya riktatām.
dṛṣtāya manyate vyarthaṁ
mānavānāṁ hi jīvanam.

Greed and material pleasure empty the treasury. Similarly, impiety turns the human form of life futile. (70)

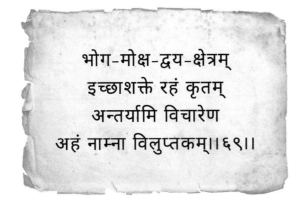

यद् भावि तद् भवत्येव
सत्यं तस्य विधानकम्।
निर्भरता सदिच्छायां
प्रेम नयनमागतम्।।७१।।

yad bhāvi tad bhavatyeva
satyaṁ tasya vidhānakam.
nirbharatā sadicchāyāṁ
prema nayanamāgatam.

The truth is, whatever obvious it will happen, that is his dispensation. With this belief, if one can surrender willingly, ecstatic love appears. (71)

कर्म तस्मैहि सेवेति
एतद् यत् स्थिर लक्ष्यकम्।
निश्चिन्त मनसा तिष्ठेत्
कर्मफलं तदर्पनम्।।७२।।

karma tasmaihi seveti
etad yat sthira lakṣyakam.
niścinta manasā tiṣṭhet
karmaphalaṁ tadarpanam.

When every work is His service, and that's the only goal of life, the mind becomes peaceful by offering all the results to him. (72)

माया-मोह-महामाया
मूलमेकं नहि द्वयम्।
नात्यमोहं गते जीवे
सदानन्दं विराजितम्।।७३।।

māyā-moha-mahāmāyā
mūlamekaṁ nahi dvayam.
nāṭyamohaṁ gate jīve
sadānandaṁ birājitam.

Illusion, delusion, and the great goddess(Mahāmāyā), all are ultimately one, not two. With her grace dramatic dilution of life settled in only eternal joy. (73)

तावदेव वहिर्ज्योतिः
यावद् अजर भावनम्
अन्तर्ज्योतिर्यथाफलं
ददातिचात्म दर्शनम्।।७४।।

tāvadeva bahirjyotiḥ
yāvad ajara bhāvanam.
antarjyotiryathāphalaṁ
dadāticātma darśanam.

Outer sight is restricted within the young age. When the inner light kindles from inside, introspection arises. (74)

फलासक्तस्य कर्त्तुश्च
कदापि नात्म-चिन्तनम्
भोगसर्वस्व संसारे
स्वचित्तनं सुदुर्लभम्।।७५।।

phalāsaktasya karttuśca
kadāpi nātma-cintanam.
bhogasarvasva saṁsāre
svacittanaṁ sudurlabham.

People with an extreme desire to the fruits of labor, never get a chance of introspection. In the worldly tempted and avarice life, self-thinking is rare. (75)

एकतो यच्छतः शुन्यम्
धनिनो भोग वाहुल्यम्।
एकेनैव लभन्ते च
धर्मिणस्तत्वमेककम्।।७६।।

ekato yacchataḥ śūnyam
dhanino bhoga vāhulyam.
ekenaiva labhante ca
dharmiṇastatvamekakam.

In material life, adding zeros after one, a person multiplies his wealth. But following the theory of 'Oneness', only an ascetic acquires 'The One' or mokṣa. (76)

साध्यंसत् साधनं प्राणः
साधकः शिव सेवकः।
विश्वासे स्वागता श्रद्धा
सञ्चाययति साधनम्।।७७।।

sādhyaṁsat sādhanaṁ prāṇaḥ
sādhakaḥ śiva sevakaḥ.
viśvāse śvāgatā śraddhā
sañcāyatī sādhanam.

A disciple of Shiva, The devotee, achieves the real truth with dedicated practice. The field of realization enlivens from belief and respect. (77)

आचारे चित्तशुद्धिः स्यात्
तच्चित्ते देव दर्शनम्।
राजसाक्षात् वहिःशुद्धौ
दैवते चित्त केवलम्।।७८।।

ācāre cittaśuddhiḥ syāt
taccitte deva darśanam.
rājasākṣāt bahiḥ śuddhau
daivate citta kevalam.

Mind purification is achieved by practicing daily rites. The God himself appears on that pure mind. To visit the king one should maintain the protocols. Similarly to realize god a pure mind is needed. (78)

आत्मज्ञानां संसारेषु
सदा साधु-समागमम्।
तेषामपि विवेकेषु
विश्व प्रेमाधिगम्यकम्।।७९।।

ātmajñānāṁ saṁsāreṣu
sadā sādhu-samāgamam.
teṣāmapi vivekeṣu
viśva premādhigamyakam.

The surroundings of Self-realized persons are always full of ascetics. With their conscience, they become the receptacle of universal love. (79)

उपायो वद्ध मुक्तेश्च
शुभकर्म सुदर्शनम्।
अनुभूतिः स्थितिर्ध्यानं
लक्ष्यमेकं हि तत्-पदम्।।८०।।

upāyo vaddha mukteśca
śubhakarma sudarśanam.
anubhūtiḥ sthitirdhyānaṁ
lakṣamekaṁ hi tat-padam.

Auspicious rituals and positive observations show the path of liberation from worldly stagnant life. Through meditation calm your emotions down, and only focus is His glorious feet. (80)

एकस्वरस्य सप्तत्वं
भावुकस्य तद् एककम्।
मन एकस्वरी कृत्य
हे जगदीश गायताम्।।८१।।

ekasvarasya saptatvaṁ
bhāvukasya tad ekakam.
mana ekasvarī kṛtya
he jagadīśa gāyatām.

Seven notes are embedded in one, a contemplative is always submerged within it. Sing the name of the lord(Jagadīś) by tuning your mind to that single note. (81)

कौशलेन तडागादेः
यथैव जलशून्यकम्।
मौनेन च मनः शक्तेः
स्थिरत्वञ्च समानकम्।।८२।।

kauśalena taḍāgādeḥ
yathaiva jalaśūnyakam.
maunena ca manaḥ śakteḥ
sthiratvañca samānakam.

The way water absorption happens using a technique from water bodies. Similarly, through the practice of being in silence, the strength and stillness of mind can be obtained. (82)

वित्तस्य सञ्चये यस्मात्
देहात्मनः सुरक्षणम्
धर्मस्य सञ्चये तस्मात्
शुद्धात्मनः सुदर्शनम्।।८३।।

vittasya sañcaye yasmāt
dehātmaṇaḥ surakṣaṇam.
dharmasya sañcaye tasmāt
śuddhātmaṇaḥ sudarśanam.

The savings of wealth is to secure the body and mind. Similarly settling the mind to auspicious practice manifests the gracious existence of the pure self. (83)

शरीर मनसोः शुद्धौ
स्वीकुर्वीत कठोरताम्।
आत्मानुभूतिः सामान्यं
संयतात्मनि च ध्रुवम्।।८४।।

śarīra manasoḥ śuddhau
svīkurvīta kaṭhoratām.
ātmānubhūtiḥ sāmānyaṁ
saṁyatātmani ca dhruvam.

Be farm to bring purity in your body-mind. With restrained mind self-realization establishes. (84)

नाम्ना जीवजगत् सृष्टिः
नाम हि लयकारणम्।
नाम्नि साधक आत्मज्ञः
जगत् भवेत् तदात्मकम्॥८५॥

nāmnā jīvajagat sṛṣṭiḥ
nāma hi layakāraṇam.
nāmni sādhaka ātmajñaḥ
jagat bhavet tadātmakam.

The world has been created by the name of the Lord. The creation dissolves in His name. The seeker obtains the self-knowledge following the name of the God, and the world unified within Him.

85

अस्ति नास्ति द्वयं सत्यम्
तत्तत् ज्ञानम् अपेक्षितम्।
अहं त्वेककमानन्दम्
अस्मीति पूर्णम् एककम्॥८६॥

asti nāsti dvayaṁ satyam
tattat jñānam apekṣitam.
ahaṁ tvekakamānandam
asmīti pūrṇam ekakam.

Existence or non-existence both are true based on particular knowledge. Realizing the true bliss the 'I' completes into the ultimate. 86

प्राणै रोरुद्यमानस्य
वहिरन्तर्यथासमम्।
विराजितं समीपस्थं
महाप्राणस्य दर्शनम्।।८७।।

prāṇai rorudyamānasya
vahirantaryathāsamam.
virājitaṁ samīpasthaṁ
mahāprāṇasya darśanam.

When profuse crying for God is equal from inside to out, you will discover that He is always with you. The eternal soul will appear to your sight. (87)

शुद्धचित्तेऽपि संस्कारम्
उत्पाटयेत् समूलकम्।
सततं चेष्टितव्यं च
यथान्तर्मुखमिन्द्रियम्।।८८।।

śuddhacitte 'api saṁskāram
utpāṭayet samūlakam.
satataṁ ceṣṭitavyaṁ ca
yathāntarmukhamindriyam.

Whatever impression has been rooted in the mind, try to uproot that with pure thoughts. Apply contentious effort to withdraw all senses from the outer world and let them rest within. (88)

सहपरिजनैर्धर्मं
कृत्वा च कारयेत् स्वयम्।
ममत्वहीनता धैर्यं
शरणागतमानन्दम्।।८९।।

sahaparijanairdharmaṁ
kṛtvā ca kārayet svayam.
mamatvahīnatā dhairyaṁ
śaraṇāgatamānandam.

Practice your regular spiritual activity along with your kin. An egoless surrender with patience, apearce as total bliss. (89)

पक्षीव मुक्तश्रृङ्खलः
वद्धमुक्तः स केवलम्
सर्वसुखं परित्यज्य
गगनम् अवलम्बनम्।।९०।।

pakṣīva muktaśṛṅkhalaḥ
vaddhamuktaḥ sa kevalam.
sarvasukhaṁ parityajya
gaganam avalambanam.

The captive spirit is always free in the same way as a broken shackle bird who leaves behind all the desires and comfort aiming at the sky. (90)

यदा भाति तद् आनन्दं
अन्तर्वही रसान्वितम्।
तद् रसे रसवांश्च त्वम्
त्यज इन्द्रिय दासताम्।।९१।।

yadā bhāti tad ānandaṁ
antarvahī rasānvitam.
tad rase rasavāṁśca tvam
tyaja indriya dāsatām.

When that ultimate bliss appears, inside and out all become full of that essence. With that very essence of bliss, you could leave the bondage of all the senses. (91)

भावहीनम् अनुष्ठाणम्
नहि धर्म सहायकम्।
पूर्णता दर्शने भोग
तृष्णादिकम् अपाकृतम्।।९२।।

bhāvahīnam anuṣṭhāṇam
nahi dharma sahāyakam.
pūrṇatā darśane bhoga
tṛṣṇādikam apākṛtam.

An activity without any spiritual feeling doesn't support your worship. The sight of completeness removes three forms of travails and suffering (tritāpa). (92)

तरङ्गोत्पत्ति-विनाशैः
समुद्रवद् विधानतः।
एकं हि न द्वितीयकं
प्रकृतिस्तद् प्रमाणकम्।।९३।।

taraṅgotpatti-vināśaiḥ
samudravad vidhānataḥ.
ekaṁ hi na dvitīyakaṁ
prakṛtistad pramāṇakam.

It is destined a wave arises also destroys within sea. So nature proves that there is only one, not two. (93)

शक्तिहीनं गुरोर्मन्त्रम्
अविश्वास्यं च वाचनम्।
श्रद्धावान् लभते ज्ञानम्,
ज्ञाने सत्यं प्रकाशितम्।।९४।।

śaktihīnaṁ gurormantram
aviśvāsyaṁ ca vācanam.
śraddhāvān labhate jñānam,
jñāne satyaṁ prakāśitam.

Never believable, the mantra that has been given by a spiritual teacher is powerless. One can only achieve the knowledge with respect and that knowledge reveals the ultimate truth. (94)

सोऽहमिति प्रभोत्वंहि
ज्ञान-भक्ति-कथा-द्वयम्।
कर्मयोगस्य तत्वञ्च
अहं हि तत् पदाश्रितम्।।९५।।

so 'hamiti prabhotvaṁhi
jñāna-bhakti-kathā-dvayam.
karmayogasya tatvañca
ahaṁ hi tat padāśritam.

"I am that" means, you are only the Lord. Devotion and knowledge are only two words. By offering the karma yogā, I take refuge to Thy lotus feet. (95)

वद्ध-जीव स्त्रितापेऽपि
परित्यजेन् न मामकम्।
प्रज्ञया शरणागत्या
माया वन्धण छेदनम्।।९६।।

vaddha-jīva stritāpe 'pi
parityajen na māmakam.
prajñayā śaraṇāgatyā
māyā vandhaṇa chedanam.

Being in three forms of travails and suffering (tritāpa), stagnant worldly lives can not avoid selfness. Only wisdom and surrender can tear the bondage of illusion (māyā). (96)

अप्रियं सहज त्याज्यम्
अन्यायं कृतवान् कथम्।
सच्चिन्तया सुकार्येन
कुर्य्यात् संयत जीवनम्।।९७।।

apriyaṁ sahaja tyājyam
anyāyaṁ kṛtavān katham.
saccintayā sukāryena
kuryyāt saṁyata jīvanam.

Effortlessly you reject whatever is unpleasant to you, then why can't reject the unjust? Restrain your life with pure thoughts and humble acts. (97)

संस्कारः कर्ममूलस्य
दूरीकरण-भावनम्।
अग्निवत् शुभकार्यञ्च
भस्मीकृत्य लुक्-चस्वयम्।।९८।।

saṁskāraḥ karmamūlasya
dūrīkaraṇa-bhāvanam.
agnivat śubhakaryañca
bhasmīkṛtya luk-casvayam.

The impression is the root of all deeds and one should eliminate the emotions. Auspicious work is like fire, it burns all impressions and gradually extinguishes itself. (98)

नामस्मरन्नहो-रात्रम्
विनये स्मारयेत् जनान्।
तत्त्वजिज्ञासुम् आलिङ्ग्य
सत् सङ्गात् सुखमागतम्॥९९॥

nāmasmarannaho-rātram
vinaye smārayet janān.
tattvajijñāsum āliṅgya
sat saṅgāt sukhamāgatam.

All the time remember His name with a meekness. By embracing the seeker of true ethos, and through a noble companion the highest happiness appears. (99)

सर्वमेव तदिच्छा वाक्
वहिरावरणी भवेत्
द्वितीय रहितं वाक्यं
प्रेम्ना स्वात्म समर्पणम्।
एकमेव जगत् सर्वम्
एकमेव च दर्शनम्॥१००॥

sarvameva tadicchā vāk
vahirāvaraṇī bhavet
dvitīya rahitaṁ vākyaṁ
premnā svātma samarpaṇam.
ekameva jagat sarvam
ekameva ca darśanam.

Everything is "His" will. Speech is only the outer veil. By surrendering to Him with divine love, speech will be beyond dual. The world is within one, and realization is in that one. (100)

सद्-वाणी शतसंख्याया एकोत्तरेण केवलम्।
एकवाक्यं महावाक्यं प्राणप्रज्ञा विधायकम्।।
सम्वन्धसेतु-तादात्म्यं यच्च वुद्धेरगोचरम्।
प्राणपरिचये-तच्च सर्वेषामेव गोचरम्।।
प्राणमयप्रयासेन लक्ष्यंस्वयम् इवागतम्।
प्राणावलम्वने नाम (जप) स्वभावरूपतां गतम्।।
प्राणप्रज्ञातदाज्ञेया प्राणं जानाति हंसकम्।
जीवमात्रं महाप्राणः तदात्मकं नयेत् ध्रुवम्।।१०१।।

sad-vāṇī śatasaṁkyāyā ekottareṇa kevalam.
ekavākyaṁ mahāvākyaṁ prāṇaprajñā vidhāyakam.
samvandhasetu-tādātmyaṁ yacca buddheragocharam.
prāṇaparicaye tacca sarveṣāmeva gocaram.
prāṇamayaprayāsena lakṣyaṁsvayam ivāgatam.
prāṇāvalambane nāma (japa) svabhāvarūpatāṁ gatam.
prāṇaprajñātadājñeyā prāṇaṁ jānāti haṁsakam.
jīvamātraṁ mahāprāṇaḥ tadātmakaṁ nayet dhruvam.

The hundred and one Sad-Vāṇis are similar to the ultimate statement (mahāvākya). That ultimate statement is the regulator of wisdom. 'Tādātmya-bhāba' (Relation of non-difference), which is beyond intellect, is like the bridge. By only knowing the life (prāṇa) that 'tādātmya bhāba' is perceived. Through the endeavor of life, the goal reveals itself. When one concentrates on breath (prāṇa), his repetition of the divine name(Japa) becomes spontaneous. Through true knowledge, one could achieve the ultimate statement, 'I am that'. Each life is only that ultimate. (101)

***

"Ma Bhagaban, Guru Bhagaban...
Pai jeno antime taba pade sthan."

Printed in Great Britain
by Amazon

80362954R00040